The Sherlock Holmes Solution

A play by

Pete Hartley

an uneasybook

ISBN: 978-1-7178-9262-1

The Sherlock Holmes Solution

A play in two acts

by Pete Hartley

Based on characters created by Sir Arthur Conan Doyle

Playing time:
approximately 120 minutes

Cover design:
Malcolm Sim as Sherlock Holmes
Photograph by Malcolm Smith

Characters:

LILY
HOLMES
WATSON
HURST
ELIZABETH
MARIA

CONTENTS

The original version of this play was first performed
21st July 1986 at The Charter Theatre, Guild Hall,
Preston, Lancashire, UK.

Produced by **Spare Parts Theatre Company**

The cast was as follows:

Elizabeth: Clita Johnrose
Lily: Christine Halsall
Holmes: Malcolm Sim
Watson: Tony Heyes
Hurst: Ian Doyle
Melissa: Susan Murphy
Ursula: Alex Newton
Maria: Katie Garment
Nurse: Barbara Fishwick
Jimmy: Ian Place
Irene: Janet Smithson

Directed by Pete Hartley

Published by New Playwrights' Network
January 1989 **ISBN** 0 863191606

This version of the play was first performed
10th February 2004 at Cardinal Newman College,
Preston
Produced by **uneasy theatre**

The cast was as follows:

Elizabeth: Jenny Park
Lily: Olivia Neville
Holmes: Pete Hartley
Watson: Lee Johnson
Hurst: Richard Jolley
Maria: Rachel Drazek

Directed by Pete Hartley

Production Note

This play can be performed with very few resources. It was originally designed for a low budget tour and a simple fluid style of acting. The first production used just two upright chairs and a handful of props, in addition to period costume.

For authenticity Holmes should not smoke an s-shaped briar nor wear a deerstalker hat, neither of which was prescribed by Conan Doyle.

Setting: London and Lancashire: July 1896

Pete Hartley

ACT ONE

Scene One: Baker Street, London. 1896

Lily enters. She is in her twenties; her appearance is one of poor working class woman. She is in a state of some agitation and nervousness but is doing her best to control it. She gives the impression she is in a busy street. It is as if she is waiting for someone - but not in order to meet them. She sees someone approaching and draws back out of sight.

Holmes and Watson cross the stage.

When they have gone, Lily re-emerges. Her focus now is upward as if looking towards a first floor window. She edges to one side and gathers up her composure, then exits.

1

Scene Two: The study of 221(b) Baker Street, London. 1896.

Holmes and Watson enter.

HOLMES: Bracing walk Watson.
WATSON: Indeed.
HOLMES: Fresh for the time of year.
WATSON: It's never fresh in Baker Street.
HOLMES: (*opens window*) That's better.
WATSON: Holmes, it's happened again.
HOLMES: Someone has rifled through your notes.
WATSON: How do you know?
HOLMES: A sandy deposit on Mrs Hudson's meticulously brushed mat. There is a similar deposit by your right foot. My Persian slipper tobacco pouch is lying on the seat of the sofa, when I distinctly remember leaving it on the arm. The sofa has been nudged by someone in a hurry. Your expression tells the rest.
WATSON: My notes - your history.
HOLMES: All will be intact.
WATSON: How do you know?
HOLMES: This is not the first time such a thing has occurred. The previous instance was shortly after you first published an account of my work. Our uninvited friend is someone who is anxious that you should not publish details of a particular case.

2

WATSON: Of course.

HOLMES: Next time you publish, issue a threat.

WATSON: A threat?

HOLMES: Say what has happened and indicate that if such an event were to reoccur you will have my full consent to tell the whole story regarding the politician, the lighthouse and the trained cormorant.

WATSON: And that, I take it, would embarrass the politician.

HOLMES: The story I could tell, Watson, would embarrass the trained cormorant.

WATSON: I don't recall a case involving a politician, a lighthouse and a trained cormorant.

HOLMES: That, my dear fellow, is because I have never related it to you. Hence you cannot write it down and our friend cannot steal it.

WATSON: Our friend, I suppose, is the politician.

HOLMES: Our friend, Watson, is the man who trained the cormorant.

WATSON: (*brings a chair and settles next to Holmes*) It sounds a fascinating case.

HOLMES: Oh it is. But I have no intention of telling you about it.

WATSON: Holmes!

HOLMES: Yet. Issue your threat, Watson, and lock your papers away more securely.

WATSON: I will.

HOLMES: We shall have a visitor.

WATSON: Shall we?

HOLMES: Young. Of impoverished background. Very weary. (*He crosses to the door.*)

Lily enters and knocks on the door. Holmes opens it.

LILY: Mr Holmes?

HOLMES: Yes.

LILY: Mr Sherlock Holmes?

HOLMES: Yes.

LILY: Help me.

HOLMES: Come in please. You're from Lancashire.

LILY: Aye.

HOLMES: Your accent. You work in a mill.

LILY: A cotton mill.

HOLMES: I observed you in the street through the window. You did not know which was my address. You lip-read the flower-seller across the street as she enlightened her customer.

LILY: That's right.

HOLMES: Lip-reading is common among mill workers.

LILY: It's the noise. From the machines.

HOLMES: Please, sit down.

LILY: Thank you. I can't pay you, Mr Holmes.

HOLMES: Have I asked for payment?

LILY: I couldn't really afford to journey here. I couldn't stay at home knowing you could help me.

HOLMES: This is my friend and colleague, Doctor Watson.

LILY: I'm Lily Strickland.

HOLMES: Mrs.

LILY: Aye, Mrs.

HOLMES: Wedding ring.

LILY: I could have wrote you a note, but you might have ignored it. Specially if it were badly wrote.

HOLMES: Pray, how can I help.

LILY:I want you to tell me what has happened to my husband.

HOLMES: Your husband?

LILY: He's gone.

HOLMES: I'm afraid that is his prerogative, Mrs Strickland.

LILY: Lost his appetite, took on extra work, then one day he just didn't come home, and nobody knows what's happened to him.

HOLMES: When?

LILY: Three week ago. He changed gradual like, over the weeks. He shifted into the special shed. Stayed later, went earlier; went dreamy.

WATSON: Dreamy?

LILY: Tired, but wide awake. Dreamy when awake, restless when asleep.

HOLMES: Yet he took on extra work.

LILY: The little bit extra he got were useful, but I didn't like the change in him. Then three week ago last Wednesday he went to work and didn't come home again.

HOLMES: And his workmates?

LILY: Can tell me naught. Mind you, they're not supposed to say ought about special shed. Jimmy never would. His foreman said he worked his shift as usual. Nobody noticed him stay, nobody saw him leave.

HOLMES: Has it occurred to you . . ?

LILY: Everything has occurred to me. I just want to know.

HOLMES: Of course.

LILY: Last Tuesday I got this note through my door.

HOLMES: Let me see. (*Reads:*) Lily, for God's sake help me. No signature. This is a woman's hand.

LILY: It's not Jimmy's writing, I know that, but when it's read to me I hear his voice in my head. My friend said perhaps somebody wrote it for him. She said only one person could help me: you.

HOLMES: I have an appointment.

WATSON: An appointment? When?

HOLMES: Now.

WATSON: With whom?

HOLMES: The gentleman on the stairs, unless I'm very much mistaken. (*returns the note to Lily*) Thank you. If you will excuse us.

LILY: But will you . . ?

Hurst enters as Holmes opens the door.

HURST: Mr Sherlock Holmes?

HOLMES: Indeed. One moment sir. Do you know this gentleman, madam?

LILY: I know who he is.

HOLMES: May I ask you sir, if you recognise this lady?

HURST: Can't say I do.

HOLMES: Certain?

HURST: Aye.

HOLMES: She works for you. Correct?

LILY: I work in his mill.

HURST: What's she doing here then?

HOLMES: A personal matter. With which I cannot help.

WATSON: Holmes!

LILY: Not at all?

HOLMES: The evidence is thin.

WATSON: That is your speciality.

HOLMES: And I have already pledged my immediate services to Mr Hurst.

LILY: I see.

WATSON: Surely you can . . .

LILY: Doesn't matter. I've tried. That's what counts.

WATSON: She's come all this way. At great personal cost.

LILY: Including my work.

HURST: Plenty of work for them that wants it. And plenty want it.

LILY: Well I knew that when I left. Goodbye Mr Holmes. Dr Watson.

HOLMES: Mrs Strickland.

WATSON: Holmes! (*Lily exits and Holmes shuts the door*) Holmes!

HOLMES: Now, Mr Hurst, a seat.

HURST: I'll stand.

HOLMES: As you wish. Mr Hurst, Watson, in addition to owning the mill in which Mrs Strickland works. . .

WATSON: Worked.

HOLMES: Also farms three hundred acres in the Forest of Bowland in Lancashire.

WATSON: And how do you know that Holmes?

HOLMES: From his letter.

HURST: Who's hexing me Holmes?

HOLMES: Ah!

HURST: Who has put a curse on me and how do I break it?

HOLMES: Who indeed?

HURST: Cattle, sheep, pigs, poultry. Dropping one by one, in rapid succession. Who is it? How? How do I stop them?

HOLMES: There is only one way to stop the criminal Mr Hurst, and that is to apprehend him.

HURST: The damage aside, you understand the delicate nature of this affair?

HOLMES: Your reputation.

HURST: In business, and socially.

HOLMES: I understand.

HURST: This is a private matter. Doesn't need to get out. Or down to the factory. You'll keep it confidential.

HOLMES: Of course.

HURST: What was that woman doing here?

HOLMES: Ah. I'm afraid that's confidential. Why do you ask?

HURST: She lives in the town. She has a tongue. But you've not taken her case?

HOLMES: No.

HURST: It's destroying me, Mr Holmes. Slowly mutilating my mind. The secrecy of it. The hidden hand mauling me.

HOLMES: It must be very worrying.

WATSON: Very.

HOLMES: How long has it worried you?

HURST: Three weeks. Come to Bowland, Mr Holmes.

HOLMES: How do the animals die?

HURST: They just stop eating. Waste away. I'm not a popular man. But who? And how? And why?

HOLMES: Return to Lancashire.

HURST: And you?

HOLMES: Shall follow on a later train.

HURST: Don't fail me Mr Holmes.

HOLMES: I shall endeavour not to.

HURST: You have my address.

HOLMES: Tomorrow at the latest. Good day.

HURST: Good day to you. (*Exits*)

WATSON: What's the matter with you? Discriminating between a rich man's cattle and a poor woman's husband?

HOLMES: (*Dashing to and fro, packing his bags*) We're going out Watson.

WATSON: Well?

HOLMES: It's not my discriminating you despise, it's the placing of my preference. Pack.

WATSON: Pack be damned.

HOLMES: Then come as you are.

WATSON: Come where?

HOLMES: To Lancashire. Can't you see that they are one and the same case?

WATSON: They are?

HOLMES: Of course. I was inclined to think so from the start. Mrs Strickland's face when she saw Hurst confirmed my theory.

WATSON: What theory is that?

HOLMES: That the evil that is at work in Mr Hurst's livestock is, or was, at work in Mrs Strickland's husband.

WATSON: And where's the evidence?

HOLMES: The evidence, Watson is where it always is.

WATSON: Where's that?

HOLMES: Waiting to be found.

WATSON: So you will be investigating her case after all?

HOLMES: But I didn't want him to see that. Please pack.

WATSON: What's the hurry?

HOLMES: I told Hurst that we would follow. I wish to precede him - at least to his mill.

WATSON: Why?

HOLMES: Because he seemed alarmed to see Lily here. Now pack, and quickly.

WATSON: I shall select a few . . . .

HOLMES: Select nothing - grab.

WATSON: Grab?

HOLMES: Grab.

WATSON: Very well, I shall grab.

HOLMES: Good.

WATSON: Selectively.

HOLMES: And Watson.

WATSON: Holmes?

HOLMES: Bring your revolver.

They leave the room, Watson hurrying after Holmes. As they circuit the stage the lighting brightens.

Scene Three: Baker Street.

Watson hails a hansom cab as Holmes forms it from two chairs. They climb in, sitting on the backrests with their feet on the seats.

HOLMES: Euston station, cabby. As fast as equestrianly possible. The blood of this case runs deep Watson.
WATSON: Oh?
HOLMES: The note that Lily Strickland had.
WATSON: A woman's hand.
HOLMES: Yes a woman's hand.

They reform the chairs to make opposite seats of a train compartment.

Scene Four: A railway carriage.

Watson, leaning out of the window, lurches as the train departs. He sits.

HOLMES: You're sulking Watson.
WATSON: All the way to Lancashire - and what have I got? And empty bag full of all the wrong things. And what about my patients?
HOLMES: You've never bothered about your patients before.
WATSON: What?
HOLMES: You haven't. Abandoning them at a moment's notice to administer to my needs. Slinging them on an already overworked locum.
WATSON: What?
HOLMES: Watson, you are a trusted friend and an excellent accomplice, but you are a less than devoted doctor.
WATSON: Holmes!
HOLMES: Well it's true isn't it? Well isn't it?
WATSON: Well - yes. But there's no need to draw attention to it.
HOLMES: There must be total honesty between us.
WATSON: There always is. On my part at least.
HOLMES: My instincts tell me I need you now more than I have ever needed you.
WATSON: And I, as always, am with you. At the expense of my patients and, no doubt, my reputation.

HOLMES: I have observed how readily you have sacrificed both for me.

WATSON: Not for you, my friend, for what you believe in. My patients suffer so that I can assist you in treating the sicknesses of society.

HOLMES: And our patient worsens by the day.

WATSON: You're not a follower of instinct, Holmes, what really troubles you?

HOLMES: The facts.

WATSON: What facts do we have?

HOLMES: That's the point. There are so few. The clumsy criminal drops his loot as he leaves. The clever one barely disturbs the dust. The brilliant one leaves footprints where he has never been, and the genius makes you follow them.

WATSON: So where now?

HOLMES: To Mr Hurst's mill.

WATSON: It will be the middle of the night when we get there.

HOLMES: Good.

Scene Five: A side street in Lancashire.

Lighting dims. They arrange the chairs to make gateposts. Holmes examines the gate.

WATSON: Holmes! The watchman returns.
HOLMES: Into the shadows, Watson. I think we have nothing to fear.
WATSON: Have you finished yet?
HOLMES: Almost.
WATSON: You've spent nearly half an hour scrutinising a locked iron gate.
HOLMES: A gate, Watson, that has been little used in recent months, but has admitted a valued delivery on a badly maintained wagon pulled by a horse with muffled hooves.
WATSON: How the deuce do you know that?
HOLMES: Our friend, I think, has returned to his brazier. Observe, Watson, the hinges. The rust pattern is complex and it has accumulated in a fashion that suggests little use. However they have been freed off and liberally oiled. Likewise the padlock, which has been tried with a succession of keys. Note the wear at points around the aperture. The user was not familiar with the correct key as he would be if he used the gate regularly. The mud, where the cobbles are missing on the inside of the gate bears the impression of a single pair of four inch thick cartwheels. This track does not line up on

either side of these cobbles - deduction, the wheel wobbled.

WATSON: The right hand wheel.

HOLMES: No, the left. These are the exit tracks. The cart entered over here. The tracks are deeper. A delivery.

WATSON: Or dispatch. In which case the cart would have been heavier as it left.

HOLMES: In which case the horse would have been walking backwards.

WATSON: Ah.

HOLMES: The horseshoe prints. But notice that the outline is indistinct. The hooves were wrapped in cloth to quieten the horse's step. The mud is baked dry. Weather records could help us date the delivery but that is not of great significance. So a secret delivery through a little used gate by night.

WATSON: How do you know it was by night?

HOLMES: There's no point silencing a horse's hooves by day, Watson.

WATSON: No, of course not.

HOLMES: Lily spoke of the 'special shed'. I need to observe the factory at work.

Elizabeth enters.

WATSON: Right. er, Holmes.

HOLMES: Good evening.

ELIZABETH: Where's Lily?

HOLMES: Lily.

ELIZABETH: I know who you are and I know what you're doing.

HOLMES: And who are you?

ELIZABETH: Where's Lily?

HOLMES: On her way home.

ELIZABETH: Aye? Right. (*Turns and exits*)

WATSON: How long do you think she'd been watching?

HOLMES: Quite possibly all night.

WATSON: What a terrifying thought.

HOLMES: Yes.

WATSON: After we have observed the factory at work, what then?

HOLMES: A cab. To Bowland.

Scene Six: *The residence of William Hurst.*

The lighting brightens as Holmes and Watson set off round the stage. Maria enters

MARIA: How do you do gentlemen?

WATSON: How do you do?

MARIA: Which one of you is Dr Watson?

WATSON: I am.

MARIA: Then you must be Mr Holmes. Delighted.

HOLMES: Honoured.

MARIA: That too.

HOLMES: I meant me, madam.

MARIA: So did I. I am the Maria Von Frindberg.

WATSON: Von . . ?

MARIA: Widowed, I'm afraid.

HOLMES: Re-married.

MARIA: Mrs Hurst.

WATSON: Mrs Hurst?

MARIA: I'm glad you are helping my husband. He is suffering so much.

WATSON: So he said.

MARIA: Suffering is good for you they say. Especially if it is self-inflicted.

WATSON: Good for the soul, perhaps.

HOLMES: Most suffering is totally bad. Even for the soul. Your house is . . . impressive.

MARIA: Mock Gothic. We have over a hundred gargoyles, and every one with its tongue out. Mock Gothic. Merrily mocking.

HOLMES: And are the gargoyles to your taste?

MARIA: My dear Mr Holmes, I'm one of them.

HOLMES: Interesting construction on the hilltop.

MARIA: A mausoleum gentlemen. Built on the site, they say of a former watchtower, some distance from the house but on higher ground.

Hurst enters.

HURST: Mr Holmes! I've sent someone to the station for you.

HOLMES: I think we were a little earlier than expected.

HURST: I see you've met my wife.

HOLMES: Indeed we have.

MARIA: We were talking about suffering.

HURST: Suffering. What is the purpose of pain Doctor?

WATSON: Pain is the body pleading.

HURST: I'm pleading.

MARIA: Mr Holmes will ease your pain, my love. They say you have extraordinary intelligence.

HOLMES: Just numerical knowledge. Every event is an equation. Show me the answer and I will attempt to find the sum.

MARIA: I do hope you arrive at the solution. You are very welcome Mr Holmes and Doctor Watson. For the moment, good evening. (*Exits*).

HURST: Something of value, gentlemen.

WATSON: Indeed.

HOLMES: Your wife has puncture marks on the inside of her right forearm.

HURST: The hypodermic needle is the wonder of the age, eh Dr Watson?

WATSON: It has its uses.

HOLMES: We must examine the victims.

HURST: Of course. As soon as you've settled into your rooms, I'll take you up onto the fells.

Scene Seven: The fields.

Hurst places the chairs back to back to make a stile, then leads Holmes and Watson through the hall where they collect their bags, and off into the body of the house. They re-enter immediately, Holmes with a walking stick.

HURST: Lancashire sirs. Gentle rolling strength. The bulk of a man but the form of a woman. Streams with so much energy to spare that they made cloth from cotton for us. This is where it all started - up here in the hills. Then we steamed our way down into the town and left the hills to the sheep again. She's a beautiful county, gentlemen. Sniff her. The air's so crisp you can snap it in your hands.

WATSON: Up here at least.

HURST: So right, Dr Watson. Towns are torrid places. And the countryside too has its horrors. My cattle.

WATSON: Look healthy enough to me.

HOLMES: (*crossing the stile*) Observe, Watson, by the fence.

HURST: She's the one I brought you to see. Thirty yard away and you can count every rib on her.

HOLMES: Watson.

WATSON: Holmes?

HOLMES: Examine that cow.

WATSON: I'm no veterinary Holmes.

HOLMES: You've just remarked how healthy it looked.

WATSON: Anyone can tell a healthy cow. You need a specialist to spot a sick one.

HOLMES: Looks ill enough to me. How many have you lost this way?

HURST: Thirty head. Dozen sheep. Close on fifty hens. Three sows.

HOLMES: Go on Watson. It's all medicine isn't it?

HURST: It's bad medicine Mr Holmes. Witchcraft. A curse.

HOLMES: Come now. We must deal in facts.

HURST: There's a so called wise woman been seen in these parts. She appeared just as this trouble began.

HOLMES: A coincidence does not constitute a crime.

HURST: There is no other explanation. I want you to prove it. Prove that it's her.

HOLMES: I will.

HURST: Good.

HOLMES: If it is true.

HURST: Make it true Mr Holmes.

HOLMES: Truth, my dear man, is like the air we breathe. We cannot create it. All we can do is demonstrate that it is there.

HURST: I need evidence. But where does a man find solid evidence for supernatural interference? Witchcraft is like the air we breathe. We cannot see it, but we feel its effects. Do you want to look at the cow?

HOLMES: You're not afraid of your stock then?

HURST: I'm a farmer.

HOLMES: And a factory owner.

HURST: I'm not afraid of using my hands.

HOLMES: I had observed that.

HURST: I can do farm work.

HOLMES: And mill work?

HURST: The farm earns my living. The mill makes money. (*He sets off for the cow.*)

HOLMES: A chicken will suffice.

HURST: Suit yourself.

WATSON: Did you not wish to examine the cow?

HOLMES: I wish to examine (*calls:*) - Mr Hurst?

HURST: Aye?

HOLMES: That building?

HURST: Stay away from it Mr Holmes. Shepherd's cottage. Dangerous place. Derelict to the point of self-demolition. I've had to fence it off. Next strong wind'll finish it. Enter that and you're not likely to come out again.

HOLMES: A place to avoid.

Hurst lays one chair against the other to make a simple hen house. He peers inside.

HURST: The hen house is a much safer place. (*He indicates something on the floor of the hen house.*) One of yesterday's casualties.

HOLMES: What do you make of that Watson?

WATSON: It's dead Holmes.

HURST: Very lean meat and very little of it. Investigate, Mr Holmes. And quickly.

HOLMES: Back to the house Watson. Bring the chicken.

Holmes and Watson exeunt.

Scene Eight: The residence of William Hurst.

They exeunt as Maria and Hurst enter, position the chairs, and sink into them. She reads from a small book.

MARIA: He's brilliant.
HURST: That's what I'm afraid of. It's a tangled mess.
MARIA: Are you sorry you let me persuade you to send for him?
HURST: You could persuade me to summon the devil, you know that. No, I'm not sorry. (*He rises and crosses to look out of the window*)
MARIA: My love. Don't worry. He'll do as we hope. Then we can rejoice together, for always.
HURST: As long as he stays away from the factory.
MARIA: My dear darling, whatever he could see there does not matter.
HURST: Of course it matters. He needs to stay up here. Where is he now?
MARIA: I don't know, I think . . .
HURST: What?
MARIA: He has gone into the town.
HURST: What?
MARIA: Some minutes ago. Fifteen, no more.
HURST: Damn! (*Exits*)

Maria exits as Holmes and Watson cross.

Scene Nine: A Street.

WATSON: Where are we going?
HOLMES: Down a sewer.
WATSON: What?
HOLMES: Down a sewer.

Scene Ten: The residence of William Hurst.

MARIA: (*At the window*). Keep going Mr Holmes. You're on the right lines I'm sure. There is a criminal in each of us. Some part that doesn't want to be found out. That's why men make great detectives. They love finding fault. They can also be unbelievably rash. Don't do anything silly William. We need Mr Holmes. We need him. (*Exits*)

Scene Eleven: A sewer.

A tunnel of green light upstage to downstage. Holmes and Watson wade on. Holmes bears a lantern.

WATSON: Is this really necessary?

HOLMES: The worst way out is often the best way in. And I think there may be additional benefits.

WATSON: Well there are certainly additional drawbacks.

HOLMES: This, I believe, puts us directly under the special shed.

WATSON: Holmes! What's that?

HOLMES: We're in a sewer Watson. Do you really want me to tell you?

WATSON: Not that - that.

HOLMES: Well done Watson. Your pocket knife please. It is, my friend, a sack.

WATSON: I can see that. (*hands Holmes the knife. Holmes cuts*)

HOLMES: Lodged against the ladder when the effluent level fell. (*He takes a handful of the contents.*)

WATSON: Well?

HOLMES: (*handing some to Watson*) Leaves.

WATSON: Leaves?

HOLMES: Chewed leaves.

WATSON: Ugh!

HOLMES: The delivery we detected earlier.

WATSON: Chewed leaves?

HOLMES: They were not chewed when they arrived.

WATSON: This is what you found in the crop of the chicken.

HOLMES: And the stomach. This is what we came in search of. We'll go up into the shed in a moment, but first let's see if we can find more.

WATSON: Must we? (*They paddle.*)

They position the chairs seat front to seat front to form a step from the sewer area into the special shed. Watson mimes raising the manhole cover and climbs from the sewer onto the chairs.

HOLMES: Give me a hand, Watson. Preferably the other one.

Watson helps Holmes out of the sewer and they step into the shed

Scene Twelve: The Special Shed.

WATSON: A weaving shed.
HOLMES: With whitewashed windows and double-locked doors, and, if I'm not very much mistaken, simple living quarters. Bed, stove.
WATSON: Bath by any chance?
HOLMES: Wash basin.
WATSON: Ah. (*He washes his hands*) Why all this inside a factory?
HOLMES: Security. This is a guardhouse. But where is the guard?
WATSON: It's some sort of experiment isn't it?
HOLMES: Problem. How to get more work out of the human worker.
WATSON: And the solution?
HOLMES: Make him super-human. Give him something that makes him feel strong though he is weak, feel fed though he is hungry. Peruvian Indian farmers discovered that if they chewed the leaves of the coca plant they could work longer and harder. If Peruvian Indian farmers, why not Lancashire millworkers? (*He opens a sack he has found.*)
WATSON: Coca leaves?
HOLMES: Powder the extract and you have .. ?
WATSON: Cocaine?
HOLMES: Cocaine.
WATSON: What does chewing the leaves do?
HOLMES: The cocaine anaesthetizes the stomach. So though the body craves for food, it feels no

hunger. One feels wide awake though one needs sleep.

WATSON: The body would waste away.

HOLMES: Increase the dosage.

WATSON: Then it would burn out.

HOLMES: (*By the manhole*) And then it would have to disappear.

WATSON: Jimmy Strickland.

HOLMES: The sewer is large. They could wait for wet weather, or flush out the boilers.

WATSON: And who are 'they'?

HOLMES: They, Watson, are who they always are.

WATSON: Who's that?

HOLMES: The enemy.

A gunshot rings out and Watson pushes Holmes aside. Another gunshot.

HOLMES: Down the sewer. (*He pushes Watson into the sewer and leaps in after him.*)

Scene Thirteen: The sewer.

HOLMES: All right?
WATSON: Yes. (*They run a little. Watson stops Holmes*) This is cowardly.
HOLMES: Yes. (*They run further*) Steady now Watson.
WATSON: Are we going back?
HOLMES: Not tonight.
WATSON: How far to the outside manhole?
HOLMES: A few yards.

They find the manhole but can't move it.

HOLMES: It's stuck. There must be something on top: a wagon or something. We'll have to go further.
WATSON: It narrows. We'll not get through.
HOLMES: Back then.
WATSON: The water level's rising.
HOLMES: And getting warmer.
WATSON: Listen. Steam.
HOLMES: Someone's emptying the boilers.

They indicate by mime that the water level is still rising. Stepping onto the chairs. They are pressed against the sewer ceiling.

WATSON: Holmes.

HOLMES: For God's sake don't say anything memorable. I'd never forgive you.

WATSON: You won't have time. This looks like it, old chap.

HOLMES: When all else fails, one thing always remains Watson.

WATSON: What's that?

HOLMES: Willpower.

WATSON: Oh wonderful.

HOLMES: Listen. It's stopped. The level's falling. (*They climb down.*)

HOLMES: Well, my friend, it seems we are fated to escape.

WATSON: Listen.

Elizabeth comes paddling along the sewer.

ELIZABETH: Evening.

WATSON: Good evening.

HOLMES: We meet again.

ELIZABETH: Name's Elizabeth.

HOLMES: Elizabeth.

WATSON: Do you live down here?

ELIZABETH: What a daft question. Does it look like I live down here?

HOLMES: Don't answer than Watson. It seems we owe you, well, a great deal

ELIZABETH: Lily's come on home.

HOLMES: I'd like to see her.

ELIZABETH: Come now. While it's dark.

HOLMES: Come along Watson, a brisk evening walk will dry us out.

The sewer effect fades as Lily enters, takes one of the chairs and crosses the stage. The others follow her, Holmes bringing the other chair. Holmes and Lily sit.

Scene Fourteen: Lily's House.

LILY: It were cruel of you to mislead me, but I can see the kindness in it. You haven't found Jimmy?

HOLMES: Not yet. What did he tell you about the special shed?

LILY: Wouldn't talk about it. Said he weren't allowed to. None of them are. Mr Holmes, I'm just a simple woman. I can't read and I can't write and I've never solved a puzzle in my life. But I've heard of you. A kind person from the church read me one of the accounts Doctor Watson had written of your marvelous adventures. So when Jimmy went and Elizabeth couldn't find him - not by any means she tried - then I thought of you. I used all my savings to come and see you, to ask for your help.

HOLMES: Your friend saved our lives.

LILY: She sent me to you.

HOLMES: Did she? How did you get into the shed?

ELIZABETH: I can change myself Mr Holmes. I can be a cat, rat, a bat.

HOLMES: Really?

ELIZABETH: Really.

HOLMES: Go on then.

ELIZABETH: I don't perform to order.

HOLMES: Hmm. And how do you live Elizabeth?

ELIZABETH: Off the land. I can look after myself. I do cures. And curses if you want em. I can make folk fertile, and make em shed a kid they don't want. I can cure your animals - if I want to. I can read your hand and the signs in the sky. I know a good person. And a bad un. And I know when your luck's changing.

HOLMES: And how did you get into the shed?

ELZABETH: He left the door open.

WATSON: He? Who is "he"?

ELIZABETH: Him that owns that place.

WATSON: Hurst?

ELIZABETH: Aye. Hurst. I watched him drain his boilers. When he left, I turned off the taps.

HOLMES: We are in your debt.

ELIZABETH: Then help Lily.

LILY: I just need to know, Mr Holmes, can you appreciate that? I just need to know. My Jimmy isn't the first. Folk setting off for work in the morning and not being seen again.

HOLMES: Setting off for work or setting out from work?

LILY: Jimmy went to work one Wednesday and I never saw him again.

ELIZABETH: Went to work in Hurst's mill. What you gonna do about him Mr Holmes?

HOLMES: For the moment, nothing. There is a puzzle here and we must play a little before we can solve it. He may well be at fault in his factory . . .

WATSON: But why poison his own cattle? Then bring you in to solve it? Then take a pot shot at you before you can come up with an answer?

HOLMES: Why indeed.? (*to Elizabeth:*) No crime, however wicked, warrants revenge.

ELIZABETH: I ain't touched them beasts Mr Holmes.

HOLMES: Someone has. And we must find out who in order to understand what is going on here. Behind every crime there is a shrouded stranger.

ELIZABETH: A shrouded stranger?

HOLMES: His face, his hands, his whole form is hidden from us. Yet we feel his blows. In essence it is the same person every crime.

ELIZABETH: Like a spirit.

HOLMES: The familiar stranger.

WATSON: Same stranger.

ELIZABETH: Different shape.

HOLMES: And it is our job . . .

WATSON: To unmask him.

HOLMES: We must go. Look after Lily.

ELIZABETH: I will.

Lily and Elizabeth exeunt

Scene Fifteen: The grounds of Hurst's residence.

HOLMES: Morning, Watson.
WATSON: Morning Holmes.
HOLMES: How was your breakfast?
WATSON: The bacon was very lean.
HOLMES: Yes. Well, the rain is clearing. Just in time.
WATSON: Just in time for what?
HOLMES: A walk in the grounds.

Holmes joins the chairs to make a bench and then exits. Watson and Maria stroll across.

WATSON: Ah Mrs Hurst. You're out early.
MARIA: I've been to the mausoleum. It's only a brief stroll.
WATSON: I didn't see you leave the house.
MARIA: No, I came round the back way. Where is your friend?
WATSON: Oh he's been having a good look round. The gardens, the stables, the tack room. All very impressive.
MARIA: Yes William is very proud of his home and his estate.
WATSON: Have you ever been to your husband's mill?
MARIA: Good heavens no. I stay away.
WATSON: Does he ever talk about his workers?

MARIA: He loves them.
WATSON: Does he?
MARIA: Help him. Won't you?
WATSON: Of course.
MARIA: Thank you. It must be wonderful to live with someone as notorious as Sherlock Holmes.
WATSON: Yes. He drives me mad.
MARIA: Does he?
WATSON: Genius can be maddening. When you're obsessed with logic and reason it leaves little space for the more humane attributes. But his heart's in the right place. I've checked.

They exeunt. Hurst and Holmes enter from opposite sides and shake hands.

HOLMES: My dear Hurst.
HURST: Mr Holmes.
HOLMES: (*Smells his own palm*) Cordite.
HURST: I'm sorry?
HOLMES: I doubt that. You've been using a firearm recently Mr Hurst.
HURST: Took a pot shot at a fox. Sniffing where it is not welcome. Now, what have you unearthed?
HOLMES: I'm interested in your factory.
HURST: That's not why you're here. Restrict your examination to the area I have asked. What about my livestock? Have you come up with an answer yet?
HOLMES: I don't think it's down to the foxes. I'd love to see the inside of your mill. But factories are intimidating places. I'd feel much safer if you were to accompany me.
Watson enters

HURST: Stay on the farm. What's happening to my livestock has nothing to do with weaving sheds. (*Exits*)

WATSON: So it was him at the factory.

HOLMES: Yes. That's why he missed.

WATSON: Because he wasn't trying to kill us, just to scare us off.

HOLMES: I've had a pleasant stroll. (*Drops to his knees*) Twice round the mausoleum. Thank heavens for the shower.

WATSON: Footprints. What do they tell you?

HOLMES: Something of vital importance.

WATSON: What?

HOLMES: Your left sole is in need of repair. Also - more people returned to the house than left it.

WATSON: What?

HOLMES: And I think it is time we heard more from Maria.

Scene Sixteen: The residence of William Hurst.

The sitting room, late afternoon. Holmes and Watson sit at the side listening to Maria.

MARIA: My childhood in Bavaria was idyllic. My father was merchant of all manner of things. Furniture, carpets, rugs, exotic things. Things from the Americas, the Middle East, the Orient. He gave me a good education - so I have always spoken English. I always wanted to come to England. My passion was the opera, the theatre. We went nearly every week. I got to know the singers, the dancers, the musicians, the magicians, the acrobats. It was there I met Heinrich - my first husband. Heinrich von Frindburg. That was his stage name. He was a high wire artist. He used to dress as an aristocrat - a count - and do a comedy routine high above the stage, sometimes walking across the stage from gallery to gallery, joking, singing and pretending to lose his balance. I loved him. But my father did not approve. Heinrich and I married in secret. My father disowned me. Not long after, Heinrich became ill - a strange illness. He just lost weight. Became distracted and dreamy. Of course he was not fit to perform - but he had to - it was our living. The public began to jeer when his act lost its sparkle. One day the abuse, and his illness was just too much.

He lost concentration and fell. His neck was broken. I was widowed and in poverty, but the acrobats took care of me, and when they went on tour, I went with them. France. Then England. Liverpool and all Lancashire. I began to sing - on stage, while the acrobats were setting up behind the curtain. That's how I met William. He was in the audience. Sent flowers to my dressing room. The next night he sent more, and on the third night he delivered them himself. He's quite a romantic beneath that brash exterior. And I love him dearly. Please help him.

HOLMES: If we can, we will.

MARIA: You can, Mr Holmes. You will. (*Exits*)

The lighting dims. Holmes repositions the chairs and sits. Watson lights an oil lamp.

WATSON: Well, Holmes, the workers in the factory, the animals on the farm - is it revenge?

HOLMES: Possibly. I can't escape the feeling that we are looking at a crack in the ceiling when the entire foundations are crumbling.

WATSON: And on what facts do you found this feeling?

HOLMES: One of us, Watson, is getting too clever for the other.

WATSON: Ha! Must be a farm worker. Coca leaves in the feed.

HOLMES: The hens and the pigs perhaps, but the cattle and the sheep out in the summer pasture? The hypodermic needle is the wonder of the age eh doctor?

WATSON: Injected? By?

HOLMES: By night.

WATSON: It's almost night now.

HOLMES: Where's my stick? Watson, I'm going out.

WATSON: Right.

HOLMES: Alone.

WATSON: Now just a minute.

HOLMES: Certainly.

WATSON: I'm coming with you.

HOLMES: No Watson, you must stay here.

WATSON: Why?

HOLMES: Because I'm going alone.

WATSON: That's a consequence of my staying, not a reason for it. Why is it that whenever we get to the crux of a case you say "Watson, I'm going out. Alone"?

HOLMES: I don't see the need to expose you to great danger.

WATSON: I like great danger. I get a thrill out of great danger. I'm used to great danger. I was a soldier - remember?

HOLMES: You were shot.

WATSON: And survived.

HOLMES: Well don't tempt providence.

WATSON: You fell over a waterfall.

HOLMES: By choice.

WATSON: Well that's not dangerous, that's damned stupid. For something to be dangerous you have to run the risk of survival.

HOLMES: I did survive.

WATSON: Well don't tempt providence.

HOLMES: Well one of us has to.

WATSON: Then both may as well.

HOLMES: May as well do what?

WATSON: I don't know, you haven't told me. You never tell me when it's dangerous.

HOLMES: That's because you would stop me.

WATSON: No I wouldn't: I'd go with you.

HOLMES: Then I wouldn't go.

WATSON: Wouldn't you?

HOLMES: No. Coming?

WATSON: I can't. If I come we don't go.

HOLMES: And the case remains unsolved. To solve or not to solve. The ability is mine; the choice is yours.

WATSON: Then go.

HOLMES: I go knowing that if ever I don't come back, there'll be someone here to say that I've gone.

WATSON: I think I know where you are going.

HOLMES: Yes, it almost seems too simple doesn't it? .

WATSON: Thank you very much.

HOLMES: No offence. The simplicity is the danger sign. The simplest means is often the most effective. Trust your judgement, and if by dawn I have not returned, follow me. And Watson. . .

WATSON: Yes?

HOLMES: Bring your revolver. (*Exits*)

WATSON: My dear friend. Even our comradeship is at the mercy of your logic. Well I suppose that's reasonable. If it wasn't you wouldn't allow it. You're right, as always. It's a selfish man who shares his danger. Go on, prowl through the darkness. I'll wait by the lantern until the light returns. Yes I know where you've gone. (*He has settled in a chair.*)

HURST: (*In spotlight*) Dangerous place that Mr Holmes.

WATSON: You've gone where you always go.
HURST: Stay away.
WATSON: Where the danger is greatest.
HURST: Dangerous to the point of self-demolition.
WATSON: Self-sacrificial suicide.
HURST: Danger. Keep out.
WATSON: Keep out of danger.
HURST: Don't go in.
WATSON: No! Don't!
HURST: Don't go in!
WATSON: To a nightmare.

Watson: sinks into sleep as Hurst turns and hammers on his door

HURST: Doctor Watson! Doctor Watson!
WATSON: God! It's dawn! (*Looks around for Holmes, then crosses to, and opens, the door.*)
HURST: Doctor Watson. The cottage.
WATSON: The shepherd's cottage.
HURST: An accident. A fire. There's a body.
WATSON: A body?
HURST: Its . . .
WATSON: Holmes!

ACT TWO

Scene One: The residence of William Hurst.

Hurst is on stage. Watson enters.

HURST: You've seen the body?
WATSON: What there is to see.
HURST: I'm very sorry.
WATSON: You're sorry are you?
HURST: Brandy?
WATSON: Neat?
HURST: Laced only with your suspicions.
WATSON: With Holmes gone it doesn't matter.
HURST: You'd better sit before you fall. Known him long?

WATSON: Is it the length of a friendship that measures its worth? Never thought of him simply as a friend.

HURST: What was he then?

WATSON: A light. Amid the criminal night.

Maria enters.

MARIA: Doctor Watson, I have just heard the terrible news. My deepest condolences.

WATSON: Thank you.

MARIA: How terrible. People will be shocked. They thought he was immortal.

WATSON: He was. He died once before you know. Fell over the falls at Reichenbach. We all thought he was dead then but he returned. Not this time. You're only immortal once.

MARIA: No, he will live on - through your writings. You must continue. You must continue to write about him. All you can remember. All you know. All that you have yet to discover. His story must go on. You will do that will you not dear Doctor?

HURST: My dear this is hardly the time to put pressure on the Doctor.

MARIA: I'm sorry. Forgive me.

WATSON: No, please. Of course you are right.

MARIA: I'm glad you think so. He was a great man and you as his closest friend and comrade can do us all a great service by sharing his successes and his setbacks. As soon as the time is right, you must tell the world exactly what has happened to him.

HURST: How exactly did he die?

WATSON: That's easy - my dear Watson - he was killed.

HURST: By the fire?

WATSON: Fire chars the skull. It doesn't smash it to pieces.

HURST: The roof has fallen in.

WATSON: Oh it looks very accidental. Put an accident under a hand lens - Watson - and you'll often find a crime.

HURST: I warned him to stay away.

WATSON: That's why he went there.

MARIA: The forbidden attraction often proves fatal.

HURST: I didn't forbid him. I just warned him.

WATSON: I'd better telegraph someone.

HURST: Who?

WATSON: His brother.

MARIA: (*Blocking Watson's way out.*) It's barely daylight Doctor. Let the news of his death age a bit. It's the only part of him that still can.

WATSON: When the telegraph is read is not important, but it should be sent without delay.

MARIA: Wait until later.

WATSON: No.

MARIA: All right. (*She moves out of his way.*) Who killed him?

WATSON: We need him to tell us that.

MARIA: We should be sure we are doing all the things he would wish us to be doing. Your comrade was a pragmatic man, Doctor, I'm sure he would want us to be active in solving the crime before we have the self-indulgent luxury of mourning his demise.

HURST: Maria!

MARIA: I'm sorry my love, it's just that I am such an admirer of the great detective that I want to be sure that we honour him in the way he would most value - by doing all we can to bring the perpetrator of the crime to justice.

WATSON: You are right.

MARIA: It is these things we should attend to before even alerting his brother. After all by broadcasting his death we may help his killer evade detection. If people at large do not know he is dead, the actions and words of his assassin may give him away.

WATSON: You are most wise.

MARIA: I have simply read and re-read all your marvelously informative accounts of his genius and methods.

WATSON: A post-mortem. A full post-mortem examination. God in heaven that will be heart-breaking but I should conduct it without further delay.

HURST: Where?

WATSON: The stables will suffice.

HURST: I'll have the body moved.

WATSON: I must supervise. (*By the door.*)

MARIA: The body. The word does not sound grand enough for such an eminent person.

HURST: On my estate. I suppose he will haunt us. We'll see him pacing the grounds, forever looking for clues as to who killed him.

Holmes crosses the stage in a dreamy motion until he is outside the door that Watson is about to open.

WATSON: I doubt it. There is no scientific evidence for haunting. Holmes wouldn't dream of doing it. (*Opens the door.*)

HOLMES: At least not until I'm dead. (*He sways. Watson catches him.*)

MARIA: (*Gasps*)

WATSON: Holmes! Holmes! (*He guides him to one of the chairs.*)

HOLMES: My dear Mr Hurst. You look as if you've seen a corpse.

HURST: I have. And I thought it was you.

HOLMES: I feel corpse-like I must admit, but I think there is sufficient evidence to prove that I am still alive - just.

MARIA: This is beyond all hope! Bravo, Mr Holmes, bravo!

HOLMES: Save your theatrical accolades Mrs Hurst, the performance is not over yet.

WATSON: You're ill my friend.

HOLMES: I need rest. Station men at the ruin. Nothing - nothing - must be touched until I have examined the scene. Nothing.

WATSON: As you wish. Now rest and let me detect your symptoms.

Watson helps Holmes off. Hurst inverts the two chairs and stacks one on top of the other to represent part of the ruin.

Scene Two: The Shepherd's Cottage.

Hurst exits. Watson enters and stands apart from Holmes who uses his walking stick to examine the ruin. Hurst enters and crosses to Watson.

HURST: Were my men helpful?

WATSON: They've just removed the body. Other than that he wouldn't let them near.

HURST: How is he?

WATSON: He seems recovered.

HOLMES: A sinister morning, Mr Hurst.

HURST: We're prone to strange mists.

HOLMES: Indeed we are.

HURST: Has yours cleared?

HOLMES: Almost.

HURST: How long have you been here?

WATSON: Almost an hour.

HURST: He's diligent. I'll give him that.

WATSON: He always is. But I've never seen him search with such scrutiny.

HOLMES: That, my dear Watson, is because I am searching for clues that I desperately want to find but fear are not here.

HURST: Shall I get the men back? Shift the stonework?

HOLMES: There is no need. It's over Watson.

WATSON: What is?

HOLMES: Everything.

HURST: Well it's wrecked now, good and proper.

HOLMES: Yes.

HURST: Ruined.

HOLMES: Indeed. You've reported the death?

HURST: I shall. As soon as you say.

WATSON: Well, who was it Holmes?

HOLMES: (*To Hurst.*) Remember Mrs Strickland who consulted me at the same time as yourself?

HURST: I do.

HOLMES: Yes, I thought you might. That was her husband.

WATSON: How could you tell?

HOLMES: By the only effects to withstand the flames. His shoes. They are the same ones he was wearing when I spoke with him.

WATSON: When was that?

HOLMES: Last night.

WATSON: Where?

HOLMES: Here. The obvious place for someone wishing to interfere with your herds by night.

However, I did not find him quite as I expected. He was in a wretched state. In the feeble glow of a lantern left beside him.

Lights dim to form a pool around the ruin.

HOLMES: He knew me; knew who I was. Addressed me by name.

HURST: How . . ?

HOLMES: Pray wait. Upstairs and down we were quite alone. The ceiling of the front room . . .

HURST: . . . had fallen through, leaving one big room right up to the rafters.

HOLMES: Correct. Suspended in the middle of this huge space - a syringe. Out of reach from every direction. He begged me to help him and told me his name: Jimmy Strickland. I told him I'd spoken with his wife, but he didn't seem interested. All he wanted was the needle.

WATSON: Cocaine?

HOLMES: I presumed so. He told me he'd worked in your mill Hurst, and that you gave them leaves to chew. To enable them to work harder.

HURST: Now, just a minute.

HOLMES: Then injections. They were all sworn to secrecy. And then they didn't need to swear. Because if they broke the secrecy no more cocaine.

HURST: This is outrageous.

HOLMES: The truth often is. He pleaded for the suspended syringe. I untied his arms, made a stirrup of my hands and lifted him up so that he could snatch the dangling needle. I understood his craving and in that moment of weakness he outwitted me, for instead of injecting himself he leaped forward and sank the solution into me.

WATSON: What?

HOLMES: I remember no more. At least not clearly. The dosage took immediate effect. A brief euphoria, then a horrid creeping sensation.

WATSON: It was cocaine.

HOLMES: No. It was not. I do not know what it was but it was not cocaine. And it was not at all pleasant: terrible nightmare images, a fire and a corpse.

WATSON: And now?

HOLMES: Now we look to our shrouded stranger. The person who committed the crime. Who was it this time? Whose face? The one we most fear to find.

WATSON: Who?

HOLMES: How many times have you heard me say that if you eliminate the impossible, whatever remains, however improbable must be the truth. The one thing that I cannot eliminate from this crime, Watson, is the inconceivable.

WATSON: You still need rest. Try again later.

HOLMES: Early in the nightmare he gave me, I saw a cat-man, fangs and claws bloody and bared, leaping at me. My stick was in my hand. I lashed out.

HURST: What are you saying, Mr Holmes?

HOLMES: I have unmasked the shrouded stranger, and found - myself. I killed Jimmy Strickland.

WATSON: Not possible.

HOLMES: That's precisely what it is Watson. I cannot find a shred of evidence to eliminate me from my own inquiry. (*Throws his stick to Watson.*) Examine it. The handle is indented and battered. It was not so last night. That is the murder weapon. What did I see next in my nightmare? (*He takes his stick back.*) An eye. Watching me, from inside the lantern. So . . .

HURST: You smashed the lantern.

HOLMES: (*Lashing out.*) Over and over again. (*Watson stops him, comforts him, and takes the stick from him.*) Mind your fingers Watson. Glass. Lantern glass.

WATSON: How did the stick escape the fire?

HOLMES: I took it with me when I ran. I discovered it this morning a few yards from the door. After dropping it, I floundered across the meadow, and a little further, until I collapsed and lay unconscious until dawn.

WATSON: You were intoxicated.

HOLMES: That's mitigation, not justification.

WATSON: Self-defence.

HOLMES: From a dream? Did he really pounce on me?

WATSON: He might have done.

HOLMES: And was there really an eye in the lantern?

WATSON: He stabbed you with a syringe. How much justification do you want?

HOLMES: I had no reason to kill him. I should not have allowed him to outwit me.

WATSON: You were not you.

HOLMES: Will you turn me in, Mr Hurst?

HURST: I think we should forget it, Mr Holmes. I think we should call it an accident.

HOLMES: And what do I do in return? Forget all I have learned about your drugged employees?

HURST: You were not asked to investigate that matter.

HOLMES: Lily Strickland might dispute that.

HURST: She is not your client.

HOLMES: My client is the truth. And the truth can be bitter can it not? You're not a fool Hurst. You know exactly what is wrong with your livestock: the poison that is at work in your labour force.

HURST: I do not poison. They appreciate the diet. I don't charge them for it. It helps them through the day.

WATSON: It must be a pretty miserable day then.

HURST: It is work. I employ nine hundred people Doctor Watson. See us all ruined would you?

HOLMES: And the special shed where you inject the Jimmy Stricklands of this world to create a contented workforce that shrivels away?

HURST: All right - it's over. I promise you. Solve this. Find out who has taken revenge on me and it will all stop. I give you my word. Before . . . before they get to Maria. Yes. I know. I've seen the wounds on her arm. She can't, or won't tell me how they got there. She denies that's what they are. She says she was scratched by the gamekeeper's dogs. I don't think so. I need to know Mr Holmes. I need to know what's happening to her.

HOLMES: Unfortunately I have done the unforgivable and can no longer regard myself as suitable for service to the public.

HURST: Forget it Holmes, forget it. A passing tramp that died in a July fire. I'll not turn you in.

HOLMES: How far does your integrity stretch, my friend?

WATSON: Not as far as my loyalty.

HOLMES: Shame on you. If you were the culprit I'd turn you in. It's your duty, Doctor.

WATSON: You never listen to my medical advice, why should I take note of your legal?

HURST: Kill your pride, Mr Holmes, and help me.

HOLMES: I cannot be the judge of my own guilt. My job is to apprehend the criminal and hand him over. Come Watson, accompany me to the police station.

HURST: My problem, Mr Holmes?

HOLMES: Remains for the moment, Mr Hurst, your own.

Holmes and Watson set off round the stage. Hurst dismantles the two chairs and places them side by side but about two feet apart. Hurst exits.

Scene Three: The river.

WATSON: Holmes, this is ridiculous. Innocent until proven guilty.

HOLMES: I cannot prove my innocence.

WATSON: You're so wrapped up in your methods that you can't apply your mind. That concoction is clouding your brain.

HOLMES: I saw it vividly.

WATSON: A dream!

HOLMES: Well go back there and find my innocence. Search through the ashes for it. I have.

WATSON: You are the brilliant one. There is a flaw - find it.

HOLMES: I can't think straight. And you are making deductions based on hopes.

WATSON: And what's wrong with that?

HOLMES: Stepping stones.

WATSON: What?

HOLMES: (*Indicating the chairs*) Do we use the stepping stones or go down to the bridge?

WATSON: The stones. A ducking would do you good. After you.

HOLMES: Thank you. (*He steps out across the stones. Watson follows.*) and yet . . (*He stops and turns which throws Watson off balance and he falls to sit in the river.*)

WATSON: Holmes!

HOLMES: There is a flaw.

WATSON: I know. I'm sitting in it. And it's damned cold.

HOLMES: The syringe! The solution in the syringe! He was desperate for it yet he emptied it all into me. Saved not a drop for himself - why?

WATSON: Because he'd been told that it wasn't cocaine, but a deadly concoction for you.

HOLMES: Exactly. A fatal mixture intended to rid them of me. Intended only for me. The Sherlock Holmes Solution.

WATSON: Plain enough.

HOLMES: (*Offering Watson his hand.*) But it didn't! I'm still here.

WATSON: No you're not. (*Pulls him in.*) You're here. (*Splashes him.*) And does this cleanse you of your guilt?

HOLMES: They never intended to kill me. Only immobilise me.

WATSON: So?

HOLMES: If the solution wasn't designed to bring about my death, what was its purpose?

WATSON: Your abduction.

HOLMES: Which with his strength and my weight he could not have managed alone. It does not rid me of my guilt Watson, but it does offer me the merest glimpse of innocence.

WATSON: Hope, you mean?

HOLMES: Yes, my dear fellow, hope. (*He splashes Watson.*) Hope. Hope. Hope.

WATSON: You're innocent Holmes. I'd wager my life on it.

HOLMES: Let's hope so. Help me up.

They stride out of the river.

WATSON: And who imprisoned Strickland?

HOLMES: I wonder. Watson, someone else arrived at the cottage last night after I did.

WATSON: To kidnap you.

HOLMES: Indeed.

WATSON: So why didn't they?

HOLMES: Because by sheer effort I managed to claw myself away from the scene and stagger downhill.

WATSON: To where?

HOLMES: To here. The river. And along the river to the place where rivers always go.

WATSON: The sea.

HOLMES: No Watson, no. Valleys. What to valleys always have?

WATSON: Hills.

HOLMES: Exactly, and on top of the hill?

WATSON: The mausoleum.

HOLMES: Where I spent the night. The safest way if you are in fear of your life: lie down among the dead.

WATSON: Since they couldn't find you, they must have killed Jimmy to shut him up.

HOLMES: I fear so. Although I may not have killed him, his death remains on my conscience.

WATSON: Are we still going to the police station?

HOLMES: No, Watson, we're going to get dry. (*They laugh.*) Then we're going to tell Mrs Strickland of the death of her husband.

They reposition the chairs then exeunt as the lights dim. Lily enters with Elizabeth.

Scene Four: Lily's house.

LILY: (*She sits then.*) Well?

HOLMES: I'm afraid I have some unpleasant news for you.

LILY: I know. He's dead.

WATSON: How could you . . ? (*Holmes stops him with a gesture.*)

HOLMES: Elizabeth told you.

LILY: Yes.

HOLMES: You get about a bit don't you Elizabeth?

ELIZABETH: I move about. By day. By night. I take different forms. I see things. I know things.

LILY: Well, I suppose I always knew he'd gone for good.

HOLMES: He'd been pumped full of cocaine, Lily. So much so that he couldn't live without it.

LILY: How did he die?

WATSON: He was . . .

HOLMES: In a fire. The old shepherd's cottage. He must have crawled in there for the night. Careless with his lantern.

LILY: But what was he doing there?

ELIZABETH: Who knows?

HOLMES: Who indeed? Mrs Strickland? (*She does not respond.*) Lily? (*Holmes mouths something to her.*)

LILY: Sorry?

HOLMES: Our deepest condolences.

LILY: Why? Why? (*She breaks down.*)

WATSON: Holmes.

HOLMES: Of course. We must leave. And I must go to London.

Lily looks up.

WATSON: London?

HOLMES: Without delay.

WATSON: And I?

HOLMES: Will tell Mr Hurst that I am still conducting my investigation, but do not, I repeat - do not - tell him where I am. I cannot delay a moment if I am to catch the one-thirteen express. I'm sorry Mrs Strickland.

LILY: You found him didn't you? That's what I asked you to do.

ELIZABETH: Come on Lily. (*They exeunt.*)

WATSON: Why London?

HOLMES: The letter.

WATSON: Letter?

HOLMES: That Lily received.

WATSON: A woman's hand.

HOLMES: Yes, a woman's hand. I think now, that I understand its meaning.

WATSON: And what does it mean?

HOLMES: It means I have solved the crime.

WATSON: Have you?

HOLMES: But not the mystery. I know how, you will confirm who, but I don't quite understand why. Though tonight I may find out.

WATSON: Tonight?

HOLMES: Yes.

They split as the lights fade. Maria and Hurst enter.

Scene Five: The residence of William Hurst.

MARIA: London?
HURST: London. That's what she said
MARIA: You must stop him.
HURST: He has half a day start.
MARIA: You must get him back.
HURST: How?
MARIA: You must. We need him here, now!
HURST: We must be patient.
MARIA: Patient? Patience is death. Patience is hell itself. I have no patience left. Now get him back.
HURST: How?
MARIA: Use his accomplice.
HURST: Dr Watson?
MARIA: I think it is time for Dr Watson to fall very, very ill.

Hurst exits. Lighting changes: it is now evening

MARIA: Dr Watson, Dr Watson!
Watson enters.
WATSON: My dear Lady, what is amiss?
MARIA: Dr Watson, please help me, I am concerned about my husband.
WATSON: Why?
MARIA: He saw something suspicious, over by the mausoleum. He went to investigate. He has been

gone some time, and has not returned. Would you go after him, Doctor?

WATSON: Of course. I'll get my revolver.

MARIA: Revolver! Oh Dr Watson take great care I pray you. Don't shoot unless you are sure of your target. Remember my husband is there.

WATSON: Fear not lady. I know friend from foe. (*Exits*)

MARIA: Do you, Doctor? Do you? (*Exits*)

Scene Six: The Mausoleum

Night. Outside the mausoleum. Blue wash. Eerie.
Cool.
Watson enters with his revolver.

WATSON: (*calling softly*) Hurst? Hurst?

Nothing happens

WATSON: (*calling softly*) Hurst are you there?

Nothing happens, then Elizabeth leaps out holding a
stick.

ELIZABETH: Dr Watson?
WATSON: Ah!
ELIZABETH: Don't shoot!
WATSON: Elizabeth!
ELIZABETH: Over here.
WATSON: What is it?
ELIZABETH: Look at this, quick.

Watson: crosses to see what she has found. Elizabeth
manoeuvres herself to be behind him.

WATSON: What? Where?
ELIZABETH: Here. (*She hits him with the stick*)

WATSON: Ah! (*He is dazed and disorientated.*) What the . . . my god . . .

Elizabeth pounces on him holding him down. He is too dazed to resist. Hurst enters with a large syringe.

HURST: Loosen his collar. (*He brings the needle to bear on Watson's neck*)

HOLMES: (*Entering*) I thought you were trying to give narcotics up, Mr Hurst?

HURST: Holmes! You're in London.

HOLMES: Examine the evidence, Mr Hurst. I think you'll find I am, in fact, here.

HURST: Well stay there or Dr Watson will never see another patient. (*He aims the needle at Watson's eye.*)

HOLMES: I see you are rather more favourably disposed towards Lancashire witches than you used to be.

HURST: Sarcasm does not become you Mr Holmes.

HOLMES: Sarcasm is but truth with a sugaring of wit to disguise the bad taste.

ELIZABETH: Settle it, Mr Hurst, settle it.

HOLMES: And dear Elizabeth, so you can change your form after all, sometimes friend, sometimes foe.

ELIZABETH: Finish it.

WATSON: (*starting to regain his senses*) What? What the deuce?

HURST: Steady Doctor. You are in considerable danger.

WATSON: What again?

HOLMES: Yes I must apologise my friend. I seem to bring danger upon you all too frequently.

WATSON: Holmes! You're in London.

HOLMES: Examine the evidence, Watson. I think you'll find I am, in fact, here.

WATSON: Where is here exactly?

HOLMES: The mausoleum. The tomb of your first wife, Mr Hurst. (*reads from the tomb.*) Susan Hurst. Dearly beloved. Died of a fever. I doubt that very much.

HURST: Be careful.

WATSON: What really killed her Holmes?

HOLMES: The most evil substance mankind has ever faced.

WATSON: Cocaine?

HOLMES: The mighty mind behind all this.

HURST: And just who would that be?

HOLMES: I think we should be mindful of the Hungarian Circus case Watson.

WATSON: I remember it well.

HOLMES: And the Hungarian Circus Clown concertina move.

WATSON: If you say so.

HOLMES: I will. Ah I think I see your second wife leaving the house Mr Hurst. She will shortly discover the trip wire I have set for her.

HURST: What?

HOLMES: Do not fear overmuch it is connected to an American Winchester firearm, they are notoriously inaccurate. Or is that just Americans in general?

HURST: Maria is in danger?

HOLMES: She has certainly taken the route I anticipated. Yes, your second wife is heading this way. And look, is that the ghost of your first wife, Susan?

HURST: What - where?
HOLMES: Now, Watson, now!

Watson grabs Hurst and Elizabeth and pulls them together like a concertina. The syringe is forced into Elizabeth's throat. Holmes rushes over and clubs Hurst with his stick. Hurst lies unconscious, Elizabeth is murmuring and restless and deeply sedated.

WATSON: So - Hurst and Elizabeth!
HOLMES: Yes, and I fear neither will have sweet dreams.
WATSON: (*with the syringe*) Cocaine.
HOLMES: (*tastes it*) Most certainly not.
WATSON: I don't understand.
HOLMES: I'll explain later. Maria is coming.
WATSON: Have you really set a trip wire for her?
HOLMES: Of course not. Now get these two out of the way - well down the hill.
WATSON: Very well.

They pull Hurst off. Watson returns to lead the disoriented Elizabeth away. Holmes remains on stage. Maria enters.

MARIA: Holmes! You're in London.
HOLMES: Examine the evidence, Mrs Hurst. I think you'll find I am, in fact, here.
MARIA: You changed your mind.
HOLMES: Not at all. I seldom do.
MARIA: You decided to deceive.
HOLMES: It seems to be the fashion round here.
MARIA: Doctor Watson . . .

HOLMES: Is fine. He was here a few moments ago.

MARIA: Oh.

HOLMES: With your husband.

MARIA: Ah.

HOLMES: And a witch.

MARIA: A witch.

HOLMES: She's - spellbound.

MARIA: And William?

HOLMES: And a little concussed.

MARIA: Concussed?

HOLMES: Don't worry. I fell sure he'll live. Unless the judge decrees otherwise.

MARIA: Judge?

HOLMES: I have to admit that your scheme is ingenious.

MARIA: My scheme?

HOLMES: There are puncture marks on your right forearm.

MARIA: The hypodermic needle is . . .

HOLMES: The wonder of our age. Your right forearm.

MARIA: Indeed.

HOLMES: Yet you are not left handed.

MARIA: It does not require a great deal of dexterity.

HOLMES: I know. I have used it myself.

MARIA: Cocaine.

HOLMES: Yes. Almost as good in the arm as a Stradivarius violin. And like the violin, it is legal, and freely available over the counter.

MARIA: Yes.

HOLMES: Which is why you need me.

MARIA: So you have the solution.

HOLMES: You intend to be the first of many who will use the narcotic as a weapon of wealth. You will spawn a dynasty of misery mongers who will become the criminal aristocracy. You have discovered that cocaine can kill.

MARIA: We have discovered that people will do anything for more cocaine. Anything. Anyone.

HOLMES: Including,

MARIA: The undefeatable . . .

HOLMES: Sherlock Holmes.

MARIA: You must admire our plan.

HOLMES: Oh I do. It is ingenious. Kidnap me, make me an addict, then release me.

MARIA: And watch you shrivel and fail. And everyone will know.

HOLMES: Because Watson will tell them.

MARIA: Parliament will be alarmed. Cocaine will be controlled. Taken out of the shops.

HOLMES: Leaving you to supply the addicts.

MARIA: That we will have created. We create an empire for ourselves through you. What we call our Sherlock Holmes Solution.

HOLMES: The concept is brilliant.

MARIA: I know. I suggested it.

HOLMES: Cocaine is freely obtainable, but to start the addiction you use . . .

MARIA: Coca leaves.

HOLMES: And Lancashire mill workers.

MARIA: Be careful Mr Holmes.

HOLMES: You've got your addicts ready and waiting. All you need now for cocaine to be made illegal and you have your fortune.

MARIA: Not just cocaine, but a whole cocktail of narcotics.

The door of the mausoleum bursts open and Lily leaps out with a syringe.

LILY: Like this one! (*He sees her just before she strikes but she stabs Holmes in the shoulder. He staggers and the two women easily force him into the mausoleum slamming and bolting the door behind them.*)

Watson enters, finds Holmes' stick and the spent syringe.

WATSON: Holmes! Holmes?

Scene Seven: The nightmare.

This scene is split between Watson's reality and Holmes' nightmare. Holmes staggers along a dreamed sewer while the two women clutch at him, clawing at him with the large Victorian syringes they hold. He draws the women after him as they hang onto the syringes.

HOLMES: I fear there will come a time, Watson, when I will need you more than I have ever needed you before.

MARIA: So Sherlock Holmes! Outwitted.

LILY: By a woman!

MARIA: Two women!

LILY: By a woman!

HOLMES: What did I see next in my nightmare?

MARIA: A new notoriety!

LILY: Sherlock Holmes, the greatest failure of them all.

HOLMES: Have you ever had one of those dreams where you know you are dreaming, but no matter what you do you cannot wake yourself up?

LILY: Every night. Every night for ever you will have one of those dreams.

HOLMES: Have you ever been asleep and awake at the same time: daydreaming a nightmare?

HURST: (*in spotlight*) Dangerous place that Mr Holmes.

WATSON: (*also in spotlight*) You've gone where you always go.

HURST: Stay away.

WATSON: Where the danger is greatest.

HURST: Dangerous to the point of self-demolition.

WATSON: Self-sacrificial suicide.

HURST: Danger. Keep out.

WATSON: Keep out of danger.

HURST: Don't go in.

WATSON: No! Don't!

HURST: Don't go in!

WATSON: To a nightmare.

Hurst exits

HOLMES: And what did I see next in my nightmare?

LILY: Watson writing volumes and volumes and volumes.

MARIA: Of empty pages.

LILY: Yes!

MARIA: A new notoriety!

LILY: Sherlock Holmes, the greatest failure of them all.

HOLMES: Have you ever had one of those dreams .
. . . .

LILY: Every night. Every night!

HOLMES: I have the solution!

LILY: In every vein.

MARIA: Every artery.

LILY: You've taken me to your heart Mr Holmes and I've poisoned it . . .

MARIA: . . and a thousand . . .

LILY:. . . . . others.

The women slink off.

WATSON: Holmes! Holmes? I must think. I must think like Holmes. He said . .

HOLMES: To solve or not to solve. The ability is mine; the choice is yours.

WATSON: Now I must solve it. I must recall everything he said and did. I can solve this. No one has watched the master at work more than I.

HOLMES: You see, Watson, but you do not observe.

WATSON: Well I will observe - retrospectively. The mausoleum.

HOLMES: I've had a pleasant stroll. (*He drops to his knees.*) Twice round the mausoleum. Thank heavens for the shower.

WATSON: Footprints. What do they tell you?

HOLMES: Something of vital importance.

WATSON: What? Why would Holmes go twice round the mausoleum?

HOLMES: Footprints.

WATSON: Footprints. Into the mausoleum. Three sets, but only two sets here. And these, these come from within the mausoleum.

HOLMES: When Maria took her walk in the grounds her footprints came from the mausoleum, but none went to it. Deduction Watson.

WATSON: There is a passageway.

HOLMES: Watson!

WATSON: From inside the mausoleum. But to where? And why?

MARIA: A mausoleum gentlemen. Built on the site, they say of a former watchtower, some distance from the house but on higher ground.

WATSON: To the house. It can only be to the house.

HOLMES: It's obvious! Follow Watson, follow fast.

WATSON: To the house!

HOLMES: And Watson.

WATSON: Yes?

HOLMES: Bring your revolver

Watson checks he has his gun, then exits.

HOLMES: Bring your revolver to put me out of this . . .

MARIA: {*Together*} misery!

LILY : {*Together*} misery!

The women leap on stage like demonic tigers. They wear gloves and each finger and thumb is a tiny syringe. They sink their claws into Holmes.

HOLMES: Search the house Watson, search every room.

MARIA: Through the stables Mr Holmes, into the coach house.

HOLMES: No! Watson!

LILY: The steeds are in harness dear drugged detective. We were, after all, expecting a sick doctor.

The two women form the coach from their chairs. Lily takes the reins and whips the steeds to life. Watson enters as if searching the house and hears the carriage rattle off.

HOLMES: I go knowing that if ever I don't come back, there'll be someone here to say that I've gone.
WATSON: I think I know where you are going.
HOLMES: It's obvious!!
WATSON: The factory. The special shed. A weaving shed.
HOLMES: With whitewashed windows and double-locked doors, and, if I'm not very much mistaken, simple living quarters. Bed, stove.
WATSON: Bath by any chance?
HOLMES: Wash basin.
WATSON: Ah. Why all this inside a factory?
HOLMES: Security. This is a guardhouse. But where is the guard?
WATSON: It's some sort of experiment isn't it?
HOLMES: No - it's a . . .
WATSON: {*Together*} Prison!
HOLMES: {*Together*} Prison!

There is a change of mood and pace in the nightmare. All exeunt except Holmes who is now gently but securely pinned down by Elizabeth. She too has a syringe. The needle is applied to Holmes' skull but instead of pushing the plunger in, she is extracting fluid from his brain and decanting it into small ceramic bottles.

ELIZABETH: You must stay out of the special shed Mr Holmes, we don't want you working out what it is really for do we? It's for you Mr Holmes, it's for you. We wanted you here by yourself, not with Doctor Watson. You mustn't have any Doctors around now must you? I'm going to drain your brain Mr Holmes. I'm going to take out all that genius and put it in my potions. I'm going to feed your fluid to a fellow with a sore head and he's going to see all sorts of sights he's never seen before. I'm going to mix it up and dissolve it down in the bottled urine of a Baker Street irregular. Diced-up detective in a pauper's piss. Penny a bottle. Solve all your problems. Take twice a day after a good book. You'll be hooked. Won't be able to put it down. Amazed by the heroine, lured by the plot, satisfied by the fatal conclusion.

Scene Eight: A street.

Watson: dashes on. He meets Lily coming the other way.

WATSON: Lily!

LILY: Why Dr Watson? What is it?

WATSON: Lily. It's Holmes. They have him.

LILY: Who has?

WATSON: Hurst, and his wife - well actually just his wife. It is she who is the mighty mind behind all this.

LILY: Mrs Hurst?

WATSON: And whoever is assisting her.

LILY: And who is assisting her?

WATSON: Elizabeth for one.

LILY: Elizabeth?

WATSON: Well she was. Listen dear lady, there is no time to lose. I think they've taken him to the factory. To the special shed. I need help.

LILY: Let me help.

WATSON: We need the Police. Where is the station?

LILY: You come into my house, Dr Watson, recover your breath and your composure. I will hasten to the police station and bring the sergeant.

WATSON: The inspector.

LILY: The inspector.

WATSON: Both.

Scene Nine: Lily's house.

LILY: Here. I have a little brandy. Steady yourself with this.

She pours him a brandy and he is about to drink it when . . .

HOLMES: (*Off.*) Don't drink it Watson! (*Enters*)

WATSON: Holmes! I thought you were in . . .

HOLMES: Yes?

WATSON:. . . toxicated.

HOLMES: That's what everyone thought. You, Elizabeth, otherwise known as Leonie the Lioness, music hall singer and Maria (*he pulls her onto the stage, her hands are bound, her mouth is gagged*) and of course, dear, poor widowed Lily Strickland, alias Melissa Crake, music hall actress and the mighty mind behind all this.

WATSON: What?

HOLMES: I did not go to London, but I did go to town. To the newspaper offices. Looking back over their advertisements and notices. Music halls and theatres. It took an hour or two but eventually I found it. The Bee, The Bear and The Lion.

WATSON: What are you talking about?

HOLMES: The meanings of their names: Melissa, Ursula, Leonie. Singers three. Impersonators. Actresses.

LILY: I injected you.

HOLMES: You thought you did. I was protected.

LILY: By what?

HOLMES: A dead chicken. Very lean meat and very little of it, but enough secreted here, beneath my jacket to absorb the hypodermic needle. Beneath that a leather vest cut from the blacksmith's apron that I took from Mr Hurst's tackle room. I knew where the attack would come for you had rehearsed it, and I had seen the prints as I went twice round the mausoleum. I simply had to make sure the blow fell in the right place.

WATSON: I imagined you to be having all sorts of nightmares.

HOLMES: I imagined them myself. They were a useful diversion while I faked intoxication and disorientation. They took me to the special shed.

WATSON: I was correct!

HOLMES: They discussed their plans to intercept you. When Lily left I easily overpowered Maria, or Ursula von Uther, as she was known in the music hall ale houses of the continent. (*he unties her gag*) Sing for us Miss Uther.

MARIA: Not tonight sir.

HOLMES: She came to Liverpool with her acrobat friends and toured the theatres and music halls of Lancashire. There she met Melissa Crake, no doubt fell into deep discussion and the Sherlock Holmes Solution was born.

MARIA: It was my idea.

LILY: But I formulated it. I made it work.

HOLMES: Well almost.

LILY: We were so close. So close.

HOLMES: Yes - ingenious I must admit.

LILY: Thank you.

HOLMES: A woman's hand.

WATSON: You wrote the letter to yourself!

HOLMES: No, Maria wrote it. They were, after all, collaborators.

MARIA: My father had dealt in coca leaves and in cocaine. When I married William we decided to try it on the workers.

HOLMES: And that's when you realised just what you could do. How I could make you immensely wealthy.

MARIA: If only we could make you fail.

LILY: It was to be my greatest performance. To become Lily Strickland, use any wretch as my husband and get you to investigate. But the case was too simple so I thought about it and realised we had to get you both to Hurst's house, then somehow get you apart.

HOLMES: That's why you started on the animals.

LILY: We had to make you suspect that you were under threat. I knew if we made it dangerous enough, you'd leave Watson behind - because you always do. How did you rumble me? How did you know?

HOLMES: Your lip-reading was very selective. Very clever of you to set up the scenario in Baker Street. Of course you knew that on completing our walk on a stuffy summer day I would open my study window. Meanwhile your music hall accomplices played the flower seller and her customer as they described my lodgings and you appeared to lip-read as I watched. Very clever. But when I later mouthed the phrase "read my lips", your eyes were deaf. And at first, when you and Mr Hurst failed to recognise each other - very theatrical - but not quite convincing enough. You do of course, know him very well, perhaps a little better than even Mrs Hurst suspects?

MARIA: What?

HOLMES: Let's leave that for another time shall we? (*To Maria:*) Your affection for William is more financial than emotional is it not? You needed him for your scheme.

LILY: My scheme.

MARIA: Which I suggested.

LILY: And I perfected.

HOLMES: And I foiled.

WATSON: I never doubted you Holmes. (*Holmes looks at him.*) Well, not for long.

HOLMES: The cruelest aspect of the whole sordid affair, is of course Jimmy Strickland, who you drugged, killed, and disposed of in the shepherd's cottage fire.

LILY: He served his purpose.

HOLMES: Almost.

MARIA: And me Mr Holmes? How did you know?

HOLMES: The needle marks on your right arm, were probably administered by an accomplice or friend. I knew from the moment we met that you were a user of narcotics. Your father, you said imported from the Americas and the Orient. Once I realised that Hurst was injecting his own livestock and that, despite his pretence, he did know Lily, then a triangle began to form in my head. As I said to Watson at the outset, his and hers were one and the same case.

WATSON: Amazing, as always, dear friend.

HOLMES: Elizabeth was the final link in the chain. She was someone with the freedom to move between town and country and communicate between the two malignant matriarchs. My supposed trip to London tested that theory. All four of you working together in one grand scheme to trap me.

WATSON: What now Holmes? The police station?

HOLMES: Without further delay.

WATSON: Right! (*Exits*)

MARIA: Mr Holmes, I must congratulate you.

LILY: Yeah, you're a right clever bugger.

HOLMES: I'll modestly accept one of those attributes.

MARIA: But this need not be an end of things. Imagine, Mr Holmes, if your mind and a mighty other one were to be in unity rather than in opposition. What then might be achieved? These divisions that we dream up - right and wrong, legal and illegal, undesirable and desirable - are simpler in theory than in practice. Right according to whom? Desirable for whom? This life we lead - it is so short, so full of sorrow, of discontent. A man like you could make a million lives less sorrowful, more contented. Especially if you had the right help.

LILY: You're wasting your time Maria. This man is impervious to female charms.

HOLMES: What are you implying dear lady?

LILY: Mr Holmes is a chess player. There is only one way beat him. Smash up the chess board.

Hurst leaps onstage, his wooden club held high, he swings it down towards Holmes' skull. Holmes slips out of the way at the last moment. Lily exits to outside, Maria to the kitchen. The two men scuffle. Holmes wrenches Hurst's club from him then jabs him on the ankles with his own stick. As Hurst writhes in pain Holmes turns to confront Maria who has returned with a syringe. Hurst grabs Holmes and puts him in an arm lock as Maria advances.

Lily enters, at the point of Watson's revolver.

LILY: Maria! Stop.

HOLMES: Watson! How timely.

WATSON: Sorry for disobeying your instructions Holmes.

HOLMES: Insubordination has its place Watson. I shan't hold it against you.

WATSON: You have one hypodermic needle, Mrs Hurst. I have six rounds in this revolver.

MARIA: It's over.

LILY: Yes. It's over. (*Hurst releases Holmes.*) Well, nearly Mr Holmes. Nearly. Nearly your greatest failure and my greatest triumph. Nearly the performance to win over the most discerning of audiences, the most perceptive of critics. I - we - nearly fooled you. Our curtain call was nearly your final bow. What a triumph that would have been - not only to outwit you - but to deceive you with the perfect fraud, a deception through disguise, to create a crime from your detection.

Fade to black.

Scene Ten: The Shepherd's Cottage.

HOLMES: Their aim, all along, was to get me to here - the Shepherd's Cottage. Jimmy Strickland was the bait. They had him prisoner up there on the hill, at the mausoleum, where Elizabeth could keep watch on the house. When she saw me leave the house - alone - she brought Jimmy here and suspended the syringe. He did his job and rendered me unconscious. The plan was then to drag me to the road, into a cart and take me to the special shed. Poor Jimmy was to be clubbed and cremated in the cottage and hence passed off as me. I would be dead then - for the second time in my career. Meanwhile they would do their worst to me in the special shed for months while you mourned my passing back in Baker Street. Then I would once again reappear but this time as a miserable shadow of my former self: an incoherent, amnesiac, and addict. They would have their victory and their fortune. But something went wrong. At some point I managed to claw myself away from here and escape into the night. But exactly when I cannot recall. Before or after Jimmy was killed? Did I kill him or did they? I will never know. It was only when, at Lily's house, I saw the ash on Elizabeth's shoes that I realised fully what was going on. Lily, Elizabeth, Maria, Hurst had to be connected. So I went to town to look up the accounts of his wedding and research the career of his actress wife. Every crime is a question Watson, and every question is a chain with a missing link. Always, always look for the link.

WATSON: Pretty dangerous this time eh Holmes?

HOLMES: A little tricky, Watson, a little tricky.

WATSON: Parts are a bit foggy, Holmes.

HOLMES: Have you a pencil and paper, Watson? (*Watson gives him a pencil and small notebook.*) I will explain all in due course. Tomorrow you will examine the addicts at the mill.

WATSON: Forbidding place. I shall be glad to get back to Baker Street. Begin writing the whole thing up.

HOLMES: No! Under no circumstances. The whole thing was geared to you creating a cocaine black market.

WATSON: Surely if it is dangerous it ought to be controlled?

HOLMES: In due course yes. But as yet the common man does not know of its abuses, and neither does the criminal. We cannot rid the world of this nightmare for ever, but by keeping this crime to ourselves we might just delay the dream for a decade or two.

WATSON: Of course, it's not the first time you've met this particular shrouded stranger is it?

HOLMES: Cocaine, you mean?

WATSON: You dabbled in your earlier years.

HOLMES: I dabbled and you lied.

WATSON: When?

HOLMES: Yesterday. When you said I never listened to your medical advice. Yes, I dabbled. Between cases. And you know why. Because I was ignorant of its powers, and because I can't abide being without work. Have a look at this. (*He hands him the sketch he has made.*)

WATSON: What is it?

HOLMES: I was wondering if, in our absence, your papers had been rifled again.

WATSON: Ah, I hope not. What's this got to do with it?

HOLMES: That is the lighthouse, that is the politician, and that . . .

WATSON: Is the trained cormorant.

HOLMES: Correct.

WATSON: Good grief. Could it do that?

HOLMES: With both legs.

WATSON: Good heavens!

Blackout

END

Notes

Cocaine was controlled by an act of Parliament passed in 1924: twenty-eight years later.

Watson mentioned the trained cormorant in *The Veiled Lodger.*

Sir Arthur Conan Doyle was educated at Stonyhurst College in the Ribble Valley region of Lancashire.

Scene locations

As mentioned in the production note (see page iii) this play can presented in a fluid manner with just two upright chairs. However, should a more elaborate representation be desired the following list of locations may aid designs:

The exterior of Baker Street London , 1896.
The study of 221b Baker Street
A Hansom cab
A railway carriage
A side street Lancashire
The interior of the residence of William Hurst
A field
A street
A sewer
The interior of the Special Shed
The interior of Lily's House
The grounds of Hurst's residence
The Shepherd's Cottage
A river
The Mausoleum
A nightmare

Schedule of properties

Persian slipper tobacco pouch
Lily's note
Holmes' bags
Watson's bags
Holmes' walking stick
Watson's service revolver
Dead chicken
Maria's small book
A lantern
Two sacks of leaves
Watson's pocket knife
An oil lamp

Elizabeth's stick
Four large syringes
Gloves with syringe finger extensions
Reins and horse whip
Small ceramic bottles
Brandy decanter and glass
Mouth gag
A wooden club
Small notebook and pencil

Also available by the same author

Making Myra

Making Myra is a play for three actors.

What made Myra Hindley into the most notorious icon of serial killing evil? Her background? Her upbringing? Ian Brady? All of these or none of them? Was there anything anyone could have done to avert the terrible crimes that sealed her fate and destroyed the lives of five families between 1963 and 1966?

Making Myra opens on 9th July 1980, the day on which Myra's younger sister Maureen died. Maureen makes her sister hunt for the reasons for her appalling offences. The encounter provides an audience with the unique opportunity to witness the bitter clash of the siblings as they scrap and argue over the events leading up to the notorious killings that took place on Saddleworth Moor.

"Probably the most well-balanced and realised depiction of Hindley we're likely to see in our lifetimes.'

Available as both an eBook and a paperback (ISBN-13: 978-1-9804-3917-2)

Will at the Tower

A play and a novel.

How the bard lost his boyhood.

He was sixteen, travelling with a companion who was suspected of being a threat to national security, and staying in the houses of religious fundamentalists.

His family and friends had been persecuted and he was uncertain about how brave he could be.

Now the authorities are closing in on his latest refuge.

The year is 1580, the place is Hoghton Tower, Lancashire.

His name was Will Shakespeare, or Shakspere, or Shakeshaft, depending on who was asking.

The play is published by *Lazybee Scripts*.

The novel is available from Amazon.

Siren and Saving Grace

Siren is a play for four females and one male. It charts the tale of an American airman based in the UK during the Second World War. The story is told from the perspectives of the two women with whom he corresponded, one in the United States and the other in England. When he fails to return from a mission over Germany, his letters from both women are returned to just one of them. The two meet up twenty years later.

Saving Grace is a play for one performer. Performed on a bare stage with no props, the play recreates the story of Grace Darling (1815 – 1842) who became internationally famous as a consequence of her actions following the wreck of the *Forfarshire* on the Farne Islands in 1838. It also depicts her desperate struggle with the storm of attention she subsequently received during her short life.

This eBook also contains the programme and background material to accompany the 2014 production of Siren, plus *Chaperone* a short fiction to mark the 70th anniversary of the Freckleton Air Disaster.

Available from the Amazon kindle store.

Drama: What it is and How to do it

This book is a no-nonsense guide to creating, rehearsing and staging drama. It focuses on all aspects of acting from your very first encounter with practical drama right through to the final bow at the end of the performance.

There is also a major section on how to direct for the stage. It contains chapters on what to expect from drama classes and workshops, and how to devise your own theatre productions. In addition, the book offers some basic definitions of drama and theatre and includes introductions to stage design and producing plays. There is a chapter on professional training and how to approach auditions.

It is an excellent guide for beginners or for more experienced actors who are looking to broaden their range of techniques or progress into directing. It features lots of simple but proven practical tips ranging from how to learn lines to coping with the morning after the closing night.

Available from the Amazon kindle store.

Ice & Lemon

A novel.

Not being able to get his luggage from the plane is the least of Dan's troubles. Heathrow is in a state of chaos. There are lifeless people everywhere but not one bears any sign of trauma or injury. Global communication freezes. London is gridlocked and burning. Mains power fails. Phones fall permanently silent. Life has simply stopped. Only those who were airborne have survived. What has happened? Are his family alive, and can he get to them? And is he as physically unscathed as it seems, or does he carry some hidden legacy of this mysterious, instantaneous catastrophe?

Ice and Lemon chronicles Dan's fraught expedition into a Lancashire blighted by extreme climate and thinly populated by desperate survivors. What he discovers there could have truly cosmic consequences.

Reader reviews:

"An excellent novel. Stunningly assured, gripping from the off."

"Brilliantly told and full of humour and pathos, dealing with grand themes on a localised level. The story moves at a tremendous pace with shocks and surprises around every corner and a truly mind blowing conclusion."

Available from the Amazon Kindle Store.

The Atheist's Prayer Book

This is a compendium of short stories in search of the super in the natural.

It is a quest to reveal the spiritual in the secular, the exceptional in the ordinary and the eternal in the momentary. Its blend of orthodox narrative and magical realism cuts into the darkness of misfortune and misadventure to intrigue the thoughtful and enchant the curious.

The prose has been compared to that of Christopher Priest, J.G. Ballard and Alan Garner, and this collection is very much in harmony with the philosophy of the latter, who has suggested that the purpose of stories is in serving *our need to make sense of the natural world and of the hidden forces in ourselves.*

Available from the Amazon Kindle Store.

Christmas Present

Seven seasonal ghost stories.

This Christmas Present is a compendium of seven short ghost stories from northern England.

These subtly told tales serve just enough chill to spice up winter evenings by the fireside or lonely commutes during the hours of darkness.

Five were first published or broadcast in the 1980s while the opening and closing tales have been crafted especially for this compilation.

Available from the Amazon Kindle Store.

About the author

Pete Hartley is based in northern England where he taught drama for thirty years as well as managing a succession of small fringe production companies specializing in creating new theatre and reworking established classics.

He has written extensively for the stage. Some fifty of his plays have been performed by professionals, amateurs and student companies. Six have won prizes, and one, *Mitigating Circumstances*, was broadcast by BBC Radio.

He has also had short stories published and broadcast and now markets his output under the moniker *uneasybooks* and blogs as *uneasywords*.

Printed in Poland
by Amazon Fulfillment
Poland Sp. z o.o., Wrocław

49645418R00063